FOOTBALL SUPERSTARS 2016

By K. C. Kelley

SCHOLASTIC

Copyright © 2016 by Scholastic Inc.

All rights reserved. Published by Scholastic Inc., *Publishers since 1920*. SCHOLASTIC and associated logos are trademarks and/or registered trademarks of Scholastic Inc.

The publisher does not have any control over and does not assume any responsibility for author or third-party websites or their content.

No part of this publication may be reproduced, stored in a retrieval system, or transmitted in any form or by any means, electronic, mechanical, photocopying, recording, or otherwise, without written permission of the publisher. For information regarding permission, write to Scholastic Inc., Attention: Permissions Department, 557 Broadway, New York, NY 10012.

ISBN 978-1-338-03275-8

10 9 8 7 6 5 4 3 2 1   16 17 18 19 20

Printed in the U.S.A. 40
First printing 2016

Book design by Rocco Melillo

Photos ©: cover background: Lukasz Libuszewski/Shutterstock, Inc.; cover main and throughout: Micra/Shutterstock, Inc.; back cover background: David Lee/Shutterstock, Inc.; back cover inset: EHStock/iStockphoto; 1: EKS/Shutterstock, Inc.; 2-3: enterlinedesign/Shutterstock, Inc.; 4 top and throughout: Zakharchenko Anna/Shutterstock, Inc.; 4 bottom background and throughout: Mark Herreid/Shutterstock, Inc.; 4 player vector and throughout: Svetlana Chebanova/Shutterstock, Inc.; 4 football and throughout: Carlos E. Santa Maria/Shutterstock, Inc.; 5: Rich Graessle/AP Images; 7: Damian Strohmeyer/AP Images; 9: Shelley Lipton/UPI/Newscom; 11: Reed Hoffmann/AP Images; 13: Andy Lyons/Getty Images; 15: Rick Scuteri/AP Images; 17: Kirby Lee-USA TODAY Sports/Reuters; 19: Greg Trott/AP Images; 21: Phelan M. EbenhackPhelan M. Ebenhack; 23: Aaron M. Sprecher/AP Images; 25: Kent Smith/AP Images; 27: Robin Alam/Icon Sportswire 164/Robin Alam/Icon Sportswire/Newscom; 29: Paul Spinelli/AP Images; 30 top: Aaron M. Sprecher/AP Images; 30 bottom: Ric Tapia/AP Images; 30-31 bottom background: enterlinedesign/Shutterstock, Inc.; 31 top: Elaine Thompson/AP Images; 31 bottom: Evan Pinkus/AP Images; 32: EKS/Shutterstock, Inc.

CONTENTS

ODELL BECKHAM JR. 4

TOM BRADY 6

ANTONIO BROWN 8

DEREK CARR 10

ANDY DALTON 12

LARRY FITZGERALD 14

TODD GURLEY 16

JULIO JONES 18

DOUG MARTIN 20

VON MILLER 22

CAM NEWTON 24

AARON RODGERS 26

J. J. WATT 28

ROOKIE REPORT 30

2015 NFL STANDINGS 32

*NOTE: STATS BOXES REFLECT CAREER TOTALS THROUGH THE 2015 NFL SEASON.

ODELL BECKHAM JR.

NEW YORK GIANTS

WIDE RECEIVER

RECEPTIONS	187
RECEIVING YARDS	2,755
TOUCHDOWN CATCHES	25

HEIGHT:	5'11"	COLLEGE:	LSU	
WEIGHT:	198	DRAFTED:	2014	

It's one thing to become famous for an amazing catch. It's another thing to become so good that people almost forget why you became famous in the first place! Odell Beckham Jr. of the New York Giants burst onto fans' screens in 2014. He made an incredible, one-handed touchdown catch that set the Internet on fire! Fans, celebrities, and fellow players sent hundreds of thousands of tweets about the circus catch. What they didn't know at the time was that the legend of Beckham was just starting.

Beckham grew up in New Orleans. He comes by his athletic talents thanks to his parents. His dad was a standout running back for Louisiana State University. His mother was a national-champion sprinter who has since coached several college track teams. When he was a kid, Beckham used to run around the LSU field with his parents.

In high school, he put all that practice to good use. He had 19 touchdowns as a senior, while also becoming one of the nation's top kickoff-return specialists. (He put Mom's speed workouts to good use there!) Instead of going to one of the out-of-state powerhouses that recruited him, he chose to stay close to home at LSU. With the Tigers, Beckham was a solid receiver, and an All-America selection as a kick returner. He ranked second in the nation in 2013 when he averaged 178.1 all-purpose yards per game. The Giants saw his speed and great hands and made him

their first-round pick in 2014. He was the 12th over selection of that year's draft.

An injury in training camp slowed Beckham's progress, and he wasn't able to play until October o his rookie season. It was worth the wait. He caught the game-winning touchdown in his first game and had 156 yards in his fourth.

Then came "The Catch." In a November game against the Dallas Cowboys, Beckham sprinted for the end zone. Quarterback Eli Manning lofted the ba toward him. At the goal line, Beckham leaped, reach behind him with one hand, and snagged the ball as fell backward for a highlight-reel TD catch. The vide went viral in moments. Beckham was an overnight superstar.

He continued on a remarkable rookie roll, finishin with 91 catches and 1,305 receiving yards, the mos ever by a player in his first 12 games. He was name the NFL Offensive Rookie of the Year.

In 2015, with all eyes on him, he started slowly, b soon picked up the pace. In November and Decemb he racked up six consecutive 100-yard games, capp by a 166-yard outing against the Miami Dolphins. P it together with his rookie season, and Beckham ha another record: most receiving yards in a player's fi two seasons (2,755). How much more would he ha if he hadn't started until October of his rookie year?

FAST FACTS!

- Even though Odell only played 12 games, he led the NFL with an average of 108.8 receiving yards in 2014.
- His six consecutive 100-yard games in 2015 set a Giants record.
- His 169 catches through his first 25 games were the most ever.

4

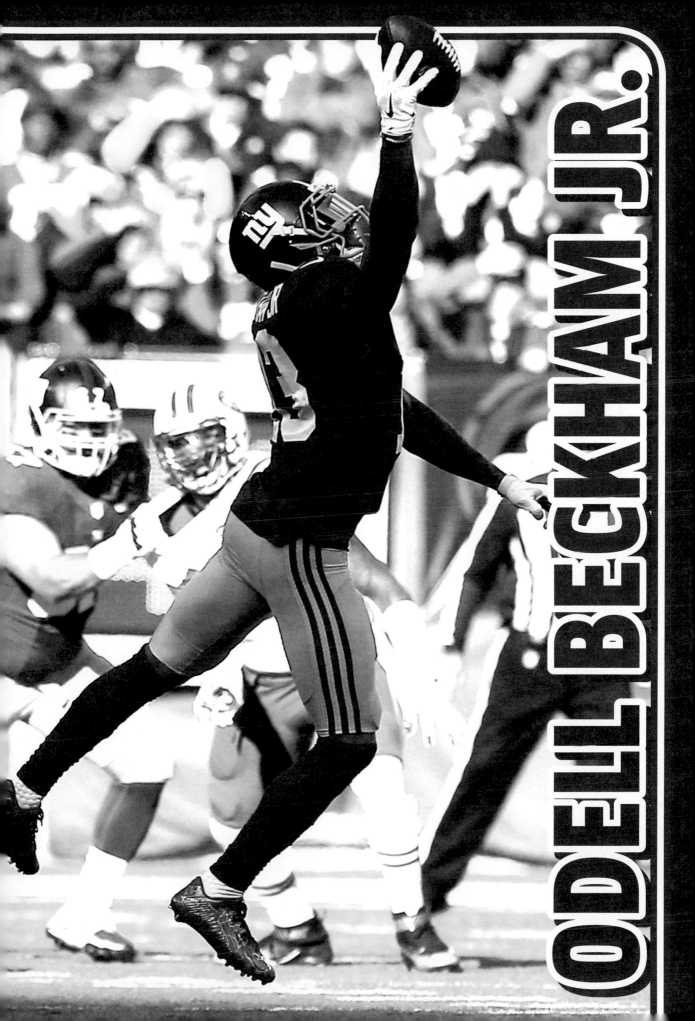

ODELL BECKHAM JR.

TOM BRADY

NEW ENGLAND PATRIOTS

HEIGHT:	6'4"	COLLEGE:	MICHIGAN	ATTEMPTS:	7,792	TOUCHDOWN PASSES:	428
				COMPLETIONS:	4,953	RUSHING YARDS:	876
WEIGHT:	225	DRAFTED:	2000	PASSING YARDS:	58,028	RUSHING TOUCHDOWNS:	17

This one page won't be nearly big enough to include all the amazing things that Tom Brady has done in his NFL career . . . but we'll try!

Brady grew up in Northern California, near San Francisco. He was a high school star, with 31 touchdown passes as a senior. He got a scholarship to Big Ten powerhouse Michigan, but found himself on the bench behind an older player. Brady burned to play, but had to wait his turn. When he got it, he made the most of it, leading Michigan to an Orange Bowl triumph.

Brady was shocked to fall all the way to the sixth round of the 2000 NFL Draft. Then he once again found himself on the bench, this time behind star quarterback Drew Bledsoe in New England for the Patriots. But early in 2001, Bledsoe was injured. Brady stepped in and once again came through. He earned the first of his 11 Pro Bowl selections. His dream season continued when he led the Patriots to their first Super Bowl championship and was named the game MVP.

A magical career was just getting started. Brady and the Patriots won a second Super Bowl after the 2003 season, and Brady was the MVP again. A victory in Super Bowl XXXIX in the 2004 season made New England back-to-back champions.

Brady was building a reputation as a real winner, a leader who competed for every yard and every point.

Working with head coach Bill Belichick, Brady and the Patriots were a machine, winning 10 or more games in 12 consecutive seasons (and at least 12 every year since 2010). They returned to two more Super Bowls but lost heartbreakers to the Giants each time. Super Bowl XLII in the 2007 season was especially painful. The Patriots just missed becoming the first team since the 1972 Miami Dolphins to go undefeated.

Brady never gave up his hopes for another title, though. In 2014, the Patriots made the Super Bowl again. Against a heavily favored Seattle team, Brady led the Patriots to a go-ahead TD with just over two minutes to go. They won 28–24, thanks to a key interception at the goal line by Brady's defensive teammate Malcolm Butler.

In winning his fourth Super Bowl (and third MVP trophy), Brady rewrote the Super Bowl record book for quarterbacks. His 37 completions in the game were a new record. His 4 TD passes gave him 13 in his career, the most ever. Of course, his most important record was a tie for most Super Bowl titles by a starting quarterback: four, with San Francisco's Joe Montana and Pittsburgh's Terry Bradshaw.

Now he has his sights set on Super Bowl title number five, and yet another amazing record.

FAST FACTS!

- Tom has started in 10 conference championship games, the most ever. His 31 playoff games are also a record.
- He set an NFL record in 2007 with 50 TD passes (later topped by Peyton Manning).
- His 5,235 passing yards in 2011 are the third-most ever.

TOM BRADY

ANTONIO BROWN

PITTSBURGH STEELERS

WIDE RECEIVER

				RECEPTIONS:	526
HEIGHT:	5'10"	COLLEGE:	CENTRAL MICHIGAN	RECEIVING YARDS:	7,093
WEIGHT:	180	DRAFTED:	2010	TOUCHDOWN CATCHES:	38

Before 2015, no NFL receiver ever caught 135 passes and totaled more than 1,800 receiving yards in a season. Then, in 2015 . . . two of them did! Antonio Brown of the Pittsburgh Steelers and Julio Jones of the Atlanta Falcons (see page 18) each accomplished that feat. For Brown, it was a season he had been working toward throughout his career. Since bursting into the top ranks of NFL pass-catchers in 2013, he's been a top target and an all-pro selection.

Brown had to overcome a rough childhood to make the NFL. He lived in a dangerous part of his hometown of Miami. His family situation was not good. He often spent weeks sleeping on the sofas of friends or relatives. He made it through those tough times and went to Central Michigan University. The school had not recruited him, so he had to go through tryouts. It was worth the effort. He was named the Mid-American Conference's Freshman of the Year for 2007, and excelled for three seasons as a receiver and punt returner. The Steelers chose him in the 2010 NFL Draft, although it was way down in the sixth round.

As a rookie, Brown was part of the Steelers' AFC championship team. He caught only 16 passes, but learned important lessons from veteran teammates such as wide receiver Hines Ward. In his second season, Brown became a starter and topped 1,000 yards receiving for the first time.

While that was a good start, he really turned on the jets in 2013. He became quarterback Ben Roethlisberger's top target, with 110 catches. He also posted a career-high (to that point!) 1,499 yards. He earned a reputation for being a do-everything receiver. Brown could outsprint a cornerback for the deep ball. But he could also take the hits after making across-the-middle catches. At 5' 10", he wasn't the biggest receiver out there, but he was one of the toughest.

In 2014, Brown got even better, leading the NFL with 129 catches and 1,698 yards. He also had a career-best 13 touchdown catches. That success made his 2015 season even more remarkable. Defenses knew that he would be the No. 1 target for Pittsburgh, but he didn't care. Brown outfoxed them all to catch 136 passes, tied with Jones for the NFL lead. His 1,834 receiving yards were the fourth-most in a season in league history.

NFL fans loved Brown so much that they chose him as Fantasy Player of the Year for 2015. So along with helping the Steelers, Brown made winners of fantasy teams around the country . . . and the world. In 2016 he hopes to add the Steelers to that list of champions.

FAST FACTS!

- Adding in punt-return yards, Antonio led the NFL with 2,074 combined net yards (rushing plus receiving plus returns) in 2015.
- He is the only player in Steelers history with more than one season of 100 catches or more.
- In a 2015 win over the Oakland Raiders, he set a club record with 284 receiving yards.

ANTONIO BROWN

DEREK CARR

OAKLAND RAIDERS

QUARTERBACK

		ATTEMPTS:	1,172	TOUCHDOWN PASSES:	53
HEIGHT: 6'3"	COLLEGE: FRESNO STATE	COMPLETIONS:	698	RUSHING YARDS:	230
WEIGHT: 214	DRAFTED: 2014	PASSING YARDS:	7,257	RUSHING TOUCHDOWNS:	0

When Derek Carr took the field as the rookie starting quarterback for the Oakland Raiders in 2014, his family was certainly pleased. Of course, it was not a new thing for the Carr family. Derek's older brother, David, had been the rookie starting QB for the Houston Texans in that team's first-ever game, back in 2002. The Carr brothers have made quite a mark on football's most important position.

Derek had a good teacher in his older brother as they grew up in Southern California. But David's move to Texas took his family with him, so Derek got his first taste of big-time high school football there. As a senior in 2008, though, he moved back to Bakersfield, California, and led his team to a 12–1 record and a championship. He earned an award as the top player in the nation among private high schools.

Derek followed in his brother's footsteps by going to Fresno State. With the Bulldogs, Derek was outstanding. He passed for 118 touchdowns in three seasons as a starter. He led the team to three bowl games, and he ranked No. 1 in the nation in several passing categories as a senior in 2013. That year, he earned the Sammy Baugh Award, given to the nation's top quarterback. One of the other players to have earned that award: David Carr, in 2001.

The Raiders chose Derek in the second round of the 2014 NFL Draft. He was expected to be the backup behind veteran Matt Schaub, but Carr's passing abili and quiet leadership skills forced the coaches to change their minds. He was given the starting job fo good before the team's opening game.

Being a rookie quarterback is a tough job, and the Raiders didn't always give Carr the help he needed. They won only three games in his first season, although he did set several team rookie passing records.

In 2015, with a full season under his belt, Carr improved in all areas. In Oakland's second game, he torched Baltimore for a career-high 351 yards, while throwing 3 TDs. Later in the year, he had a pair of 4-touchdown games. His 32 total TD passes put hin among the NFL's top 10, a good showing for a youn passer. In fact, in Carr's first two seasons, his total of 53 TDs is second only to the great Dan Marino, who had 68 in 1983–84. Take that Peyton Manning, Russell Wilson, and Cam Newton!

More importantly, the Raiders more than doubled their victory total from 2014, winning seven times i 2015. Carr's continued improvement points to a sol future for yet another Carr brother in the NFL!

FAST FACTS!

- Derek wears No. 4 in honor of his favorite player, Pro Football Hall of Fame quarterback Brett Favre.
- In 2013, Derek's 50 touchdown passes and 454 completions were the most in the highest level of college football.
- He was selected to the Pro Bowl in the 2015 season.

DEREK CARR

ANDY DALTON

CINCINNATI BENGALS

QUARTERBACK

			2,497	12
HEIGHT: 6'2"	COLLEGE: TEXAS CHRISTIAN		1,556	7
WEIGHT: 215	DRAFTED: 2011		18,008	14

So close and yet so far: That sums up Andy Dalton's career . . . to this point. The talented passer has led the Cincinnati Bengals to five consecutive winning seasons. While playoff losses have brought disappointment, Dalton's performance promises good things for the Bengals' future.

Dalton grew up in Katy, Texas, where his high school team was undefeated when he was the senior quarterback. He moved on to Texas Christian, where he became a national superstar. He wrapped up a great college career with a Rose Bowl win and a 13–0 record in his senior season in 2010. The Horned Frogs finished the year ranked No. 2 in the country, and Dalton became the school's all-time leader in pass attempts, completions, yards, and touchdowns. He was a finalist for most of the big college awards for quarterbacks and even finished in the top 10 in the Heisman Trophy voting.

All those records earned him a second-round selection by the Cincinnati Bengals, who made him the starter as a rookie in 2011. He guided the team to a 9–7 record and a playoff berth. Though the Bengals lost their first-round game to Houston, they were building a team that could easily hope for more.

In each of the next three seasons, Dalton led the Bengals to at least 10 wins. He was not a superstar, but he did all the right things, including showing fiery leadership and a great come-from-behind ability. In 2013, he posted career highs with 33 touchdown passes and 4,293 passing yards.

In each of those seasons, however, the Bengals lost in the opening round of the playoffs. However, as 2015 began, Dalton and the Bengals were putting it a together. They started the season with an eight-game winning streak. Dalton was on fire, with 18 TD passe and only 4 interceptions in those eight games. In a win over Baltimore, he passed for a career-high 383 yards. Dalton had never played better, and Cincinnati fans hoped that it would be the year to break the playoff jinx.

After an upset loss to Houston and a close loss to the favored Arizona Cardinals, the Bengals won twice more. Then, during a game against the Pittsburgh Steelers, Dalton suffered a broken hand. Without the leader, the Bengals lost. AJ McCarron stepped in with help from Dalton on the sidelines. Cincinnati finished at a solid 12–4, but once again fell in the first round of the playoffs with another loss to the Steelers. A frustrated Dalton could only watch, his arm in a sling.

The redheaded quarterback will be back in action in 2016, hoping to continue the Bengals' string of winning seasons . . . but this time to add at least one more win in the playoffs.

FAST FACTS!

- Andy's 5 touchdown passes in a 2013 win over the New York Jets set a career high.
- His 42 wins as a starter at Texas Christian broke the school record previously held by legendary passer "Slingin'" Sammy Baugh.
- Andy was named the Offensive MVP of the 2011 Rose Bowl when TC beat Wisconsin.

ANDY DALTON

LARRY FITZGERALD

ARIZONA CARDINALS

WIDE RECEIVER

					RECEPTIONS	1,018
HEIGHT:	6'3"	COLLEGE:	PITTSBURGH		RECEIVING YARDS	13,366
WEIGHT:	218	DRAFTED:	2004		TOUCHDOWN CATCHES	98

Was it the play of the year in the 2015 season? It was certainly right up there as one of the most dramatic. In the Arizona Cardinals' NFC Divisional Playoff Game against the Green Bay Packers, Larry Fitzgerald showed why he has been one of the NFL's most dependable big-play receivers. Fitzgerald took the first pass in overtime from quarterback Carson Palmer and turned it into a 75-yard romp, evading several tacklers and still showing pretty good speed for a 32-year-old! Two plays later, he took an inside shuffle pass and bounded into the end zone. Game over. The Cardinals won!

The road to that big play started for Fitzgerald in Minneapolis, where he grew up. He played his final high school season in Virginia, hoping to gain extra experience. Heavily recruited, he chose the University of Pittsburgh. Though he only played there for two seasons, he certainly made his mark. His 22 touchdown catches and 1,672 receiving yards in 2003 led the highest level of college football. He won the Biletnikoff Award as the nation's top wide receiver, and earned All-America honors. He was the runner-up for the Heisman Trophy behind Oklahoma QB Jason White.

Although he was only 20 years old during his final season at Pittsburgh, Fitzgerald showed that he was ready for the NFL. The Cardinals selected him with the third overall pick in 2004. By his second season he was a Pro Bowl player and led the NFL with 103 catches. By 2008, the Cardinals were one of the NFL best teams—and Fitzgerald was a big reason for the success.

In 2009, Fitzgerald became the youngest player ever to reach 7,000 career receiving yards; in 2012 he became the second-youngest to make it to 10,00 yards. But receivers need one thing more than any other: a quarterback to get them the ball. After War left in 2009, Fitzgerald's numbers dropped. Arizona went through a string of passers while Fitzgerald battled a succession of injuries that left him at less than 100 percent.

In 2013, the strong-armed Carson Palmer joined Cardinals. By 2015, Palmer and Fitzgerald perfected their connection. That year, Fitzgerald's yardage tot jumped by more than 400 yards from 2014, and his TDs went from 2 to 9. His reception total nearly doubled.

Arizona reached the playoffs with a 13–3 record. That's when Fitzgerald pulled off his overtime heroi against the Packers. Arizona couldn't overcome the Carolina Panthers the following week in the conference title game. However, with Fitzgerald and Palmer playing together so well, there should be m chances for playoff plays in both their futures.

FAST FACTS!

- Larry led the NFL in touchdown catches in 2008 and 2009.
- He has been named to the Pro Bowl nine times, including the 2015 season.
- At Pittsburgh, he was the Walter Camp National Player of the Ye for 2003.

LARRY FITZGERALD

TODD GURLEY

LOS ANGELES RAMS

RUNNING BACK

			RUSHING ATTEMPTS:	229	RECEPTIONS: 21
HEIGHT: 6'1"	COLLEGE: GEORGIA		RUSHING YARDS:	1,106	RECEIVING YARDS: 18
WEIGHT: 226	DRAFTED: 2015		RUSHING TOUCHDOWNS:	10	TOUCHDOWN CATCHES: 0

There are fast starts . . . and then there is what Todd Gurley did in 2015. The Los Angeles Rams' rookie earned the starting spot in his fourth NFL game. The Rams are probably wondering why they waited so long! Beginning with his 146 yards against the Arizona Cardinals in Week 4, Gurley posted four consecutive 100-yard rushing games. His 566 yards in that stretch marked the most ever by a player in his first four NFL starts. It was a powerful statement that fans might just be looking at the league's next great running back.

Fast is nothing new for Gurley. In his North Carolina high school, he was one of the top sprinters and hurdlers in the country. He ran for Team USA at international youth events. On the football field, he used that speed to run for 2,600 yards and 38 touchdowns as a senior. His team won the state championship for his division, too.

Many colleges wanted him to play for them, but he picked the University of Georgia. Although not a starter right away, he soon grabbed the No. 1 spot. In 14 games in 2012, Gurley racked up 1,385 yards and scored 17 touchdowns. Such a performance is rare for a freshman. He was an All-Southeastern Conference choice and a Freshman All-America selection.

Gurley's second season at Georgia was solid, but with defenses concentrating on stopping him, his yardage total was down a bit. (He did score 16 more TDs, including 6 on receptions.) He hit a real speed bump, though, as a junior. Some experts were picki him as a Heisman Trophy candidate, but he was suspended from the team for four games. Gurley ha been paid money for his autograph on items, which is against NCAA rules. When he was allowed back, he badly hurt his knee. Gurley's fast-moving college career was over.

The Rams saw enough in Gurley's stats and skills however, to make him the 10th overall pick in the 2015 NFL Draft. His knee still bothered him as the season began, so he watched from the sidelines. By the end of September, he was ready. After a few carries as a backup, he started on October 4 against the Arizona Cardinals.

Gurley continued to use his speed, but it was his power and cutting ability that really opened defende eyes. In 2016, the Rams moved from St. Louis to L Angeles, the home of many celebrities. Gurley figur to be one of the biggest stars in town!

FAST FACTS!

- Fantasy star: Todd was only the second rookie since 2000 with 15- fantasy points in four consecutive games.
- He was named to the Pro Bowl in his rookie season in 2015.
- His 44 total TDs at Georgia are the second-most in school history

TODD GURLEY

JULIO JONES

ATLANTA FALCONS

	414
	6,201
	34

HEIGHT:	6'4"	COLLEGE:	ALABAMA
WEIGHT:	220	DRAFTED:	2011

Combine a sprinter's speed, a basketball player's leaping ability, great hands, and intense focus, and you've got the recipe for a superstar. Or you could just be describing Julio Jones. The Atlanta Falcons' all-pro pass catcher has shown off all those skills and more in becoming one of the most successful players in the game at any position.

Jones grew up in Alabama and, believe it or not, he was a running back when he began his high school career. He also played basketball and was a sprinter and jumper in track and field. A new football coach switched up things and moved Jones to receiver, where his height could be used well. By the time he was a senior, he was a top-rated receiver. He chose to stay close to home and go to the University of Alabama. Two years later, Alabama won the national championship with Jones as the team's No. 1 wideout.

How much did the Falcons want him in the 2011 NFL Draft? They traded five other draft picks to move up 21 spots in the first round. They selected Jones with the sixth overall selection.

Atlanta quickly learned it made the right choice. Jones started nearly every game as a rookie and caught 54 passes, including 8 for touchdowns. He helped the Falcons reach the playoffs. In 2012, they did it again. Jones upped his TD total to 10 and earned his first Pro Bowl selection. In Atlanta's two playoff games that season, including a loss to the S Francisco 49ers in the NFC Championship Game, h had 17 total catches, including a pair of touchdowns.

Jones missed most of the 2013 season with a broken foot. But after a long summer of working o and getting healthy, he came back better than ever 2014. He topped 100 catches for the first time, with 104 receptions for 1,593 yards.

That success was just the opening act for 2015, however. Great players succeed even when everyon knows they're going to get the ball. Jones entered 2015 as the Falcons' main target in the passing ga That didn't matter to him. He flew out of the box, reaching at least 135 receiving yards in his first thr games while scoring 4 touchdowns and catching 3 passes in all. He didn't keep up that amazing pace, course, but he did end the season tied for the NFL with 136 catches. His total of 1,871 yards receiving was second in NFL history only to Calvin Johnson' record 1,964 yards in 2012. One big highlight was 70-yard TD catch in the Falcons' win over the Caro Panthers—Carolina's only regular-season loss tha year.

Jones is fine with the records, but team wins—a championship—remain his main goals. With his s it could just be a matter of time.

FAST FACTS!

- Julio averaged 116.9 receiving yards per game in 2015.
- His 259 receiving yards against the Green Bay Packers in 2014 set a Falcons' single-game record.
- His full name is Quintorris Lopez Jones; "Julio" is a nickname!

DOUG MARTIN

TAMPA BAY BUCCANEERS

RUNNING BACK

		868	10
HEIGHT: 5'9"	COLLEGE: BOISE STATE	3,806	87
WEIGHT: 223	DRAFTED: 2012	20	2

The term "flash in the pan" means something that is a big hit for a very short time . . . but then is quickly forgotten. Doug Martin almost became one of those stories, but he bounced back in 2015 to become one of the NFL's most feared runners.

Martin grew up in Stockton, California, where he was a football and track star in high school. He scored 32 touchdowns combined in his junior and senior seasons. He moved on to Boise State as that school rose in the college ranks. His 48 total touchdowns are among the most ever at the school. He showed off his speed when he set a school record by returning a kickoff 100 yards for a touchdown. His senior year in 2011 was his best, as he scored 19 times. The Tampa Bay Buccaneers made him a first-round draft pick in 2012.

Then came the flash. Martin burst onto NFL fans' radar—and especially fantasy fans' radar—with a marvelous game against the Oakland Raiders in his rookie season. He ran for 251 yards and scored 4 touchdowns in the Buccaneers' 42–32 win at Oakland. It was one of the best games by any back that year. He had four other 100-yard rushing games that season and ended the year with 12 touchdowns. And he made the Pro Bowl.

But then the flash turned to a flicker. In 2013 and 2014, Martin's numbers fell dramatically. He misse some games in 2013 with an injury, too. He gained fewer than 500 yards on the ground in each of thos seasons, and caught only 25 total passes. Fantasy fans were disappointed, but no more so than Marti

He kept working and, fully healthy in 2015, he bounced back . . . big-time!

Starting in Week 4, Martin had three consecutive 100-yard rushing games. Against the Philadelphia Eagles in Week 11, he nearly matched his amazing rookie highlight with a 235-yard performance. The yards kept piling up. As the end of the season neared, his teammates were hoping they could hel him win the NFL rushing title, something no Tampa Bay player had ever done. In the end, Martin finish second, just 83 yards behind Adrian Peterson of th Minnesota Vikings. Martin was named to his first all-pro team, and he earned his second Pro Bowl berth. With a new contract for 2016 and beyond, and having proved he's more than a flash in the pa Martin expects to keep sizzling!

FAST FACTS!

- Doug was second in the NFL with 288 rushing attempts in 2015.
- One of his nicknames is "Muscle Hamster." He hates it! He gave himself a new one in 2015: "Dougernaut."
- In college, he filled in at cornerback for some games and forced a fumble!

DOUG MARTIN

VON MILLER

DENVER BRONCOS

LINEBACKER

			TACKLES	210	FORCED FUMBLES	
HEIGHT: 6'3"	COLLEGE: TEXAS A&M	SACKS	60	FUMBLES RECOVERED	
WEIGHT: 250	DRAFTED: 2011	INTERCEPTIONS	1	TOUCHDOWNS	

The Denver Broncos missed the playoffs every year from 2006 through 2010. That was their longest postseason drought since the 1970s. Then they drafted linebacker Von Miller in 2011. They've made the playoffs every year since, capped by a win in Super Bowl 50 in the 2015 season. Coincidence? Probably not.

Miller grew up in Texas, where his standout play in high school got a lot of attention from colleges. Still, he was not a top-level recruit. He was 6' 3", but "only" 210 pounds. Was he a small linebacker or should he play defensive end? Texas A&M assistant coach Stan Eggen believed Miller could be a great player. He told the young man that he could earn a degree in "sackology." Miller was convinced, and he became a star with the Aggies. He had 33 sacks in four seasons, including an NCAA-best 17 sacks in 2009. He was an All-America selection in 2010.

In the spring of 2011, the Broncos made Miller the No. 2 overall pick of the NFL Draft. There was no more doubt: Miller became an impact player at linebacker. In his rookie season, he and his defensive teammates helped the Broncos reach the playoffs for the first time since 2005. He had 11.5 sacks and forced 3 fumbles while playing dominating defense against both the run and the pass. Miller was named the NFL Defensive Rookie of the Year.

In 2012, Miller's attacks on passers increased. He posted a career-best 18.5 sacks, including a pair of games with 3 sacks each. He also scored his first

career touchdown when he returned an interception 26 yards in a win over Tampa Bay.

Late in the 2013 season, Miller suffered a knee injury. Denver went on to win the conference championship, but then Miller had to watch as his teammates got smacked around by the Seattle Seahawks in Super Bowl XLVIII. Waiting around to was tough for such a competitive guy. But he fough back and returned with his third Pro Bowl season i 2014. That year, the team fell short in the AFC play

By 2015, it was clear that defense would win the for Denver, and that put Miller in the thick of the ac again. He made the Pro Bowl for the fourth time an led Denver to the No. 1 ranking among NFL defens After shutting down the New England Patriots in th AFC Championship Game, Miller and his teammate faced the high-scoring Carolina Panthers in the Su Bowl. Carolina was led by quarterback Cam Newto the league's Most Valuable Player that season.

Miller set the tone for the game early. In the first quarter, he swarmed past a blocker and sacked Ne near the goal line. As he did, he swatted the ball aw Denver recovered the fumble in the end zone for a touchdown. Late in the game, as Carolina was tryir to claw back, Miller did it again, strip-sacking New deep in Panthers' territory. A few plays later, Denve scored again, clinching the victory—and the Super Bowl MVP trophy for Miller!

FAST FACTS!

- Von was the fourth linebacker to be named the Super Bowl MVP. The others: Dallas's Chuck Howley (Super Bowl V), Baltimore's Ray Le (XXXV), and Seattle's Malcolm Smith (XLVIII).
- At Texas A&M, Von won the Butkus Award as the nation's top linebacker for 2010.

VON MILLER

CAM NEWTON

CAROLINA PANTHERS
QUARTERBACK

		ATTEMPTS: 2,419	TOUCHDOWN PASSES: 117
HEIGHT: 6'5"	COLLEGE: AUBURN	COMPLETIONS: 1,440	RUSHING YARDS: 3,207
WEIGHT: 245	DRAFTED: 2011	PASSING YARDS: 18,263	RUSHING TOUCHDOWNS: 43

He can run. He can pass. He can lead. He can fly? It only seems like Cam Newton can fly, but he surely can do all those other things, and more. The Carolina Panthers' awesomely talented quarterback has been a star since his college days at Auburn, but in 2015 he rocketed even further.

Newton has covered a lot of ground in his NFL career, but getting there took a lot of travel, too. He grew up near Atlanta and, after growing quite a bit during high school, became a top quarterback. Many schools recruited him, but he chose Florida. The Gators, however, had another QB ahead of him—Tim Tebow. Newton waited and learned. He thought he would get his shot, but Tebow kept the starting job. The waiting was hard, and Newton made some mistakes in school and with the police.

He decided that a change of scenery would help, so he played a year in junior college. Then he moved on to Auburn. He showed off his multiple skills in his first game there, passing for 3 touchdowns and running 71 yards for another! He led the Tigers to a perfect season, but the signature game was against archrival Alabama. Auburn trailed 24–0 before Newton took over. He threw 3 TD passes, ran for another, and Auburn came back to win 28–27. Newton's outstanding play earned him the Heisman Trophy. He capped off his season by leading Auburn to a victory over Oregon for the national championship.

To no one's surprise, Newton was the No. 1 overall pick of the 2011 NFL Draft. Once again, he got off to a fast start, setting an NFL rookie record in his very first game with 422 passing yards—a record he beat the next week by 10 yards! As the season went on, he learned more and more how to play in the NFL. Defenses also learned that he would be tough to stop. His 14 rushing touchdowns that season set a new record for quarterbacks, and he had 4,051 passing yards. He was an easy pick for NFL Offensive Rookie of the Year.

Over the next three seasons, Newton and the Panthers kept trying to improve, but even all his skill could not get the team over the top. Carolina won the NFC South in 2013 and 2014, but lost in the division round of the playoffs.

Newton put all that behind him in a magical 2015 season. The Panthers added a powerful defense to complement their QB's skills. They won their first 14 games that year! Newton had a pair of games with 5 touchdown passes. He ran for 10 TDs and, in just his fifth season, equaled the NFL career mark for rushing scores by a quarterback. Carolina finished the regular season at 15–1, the team's best record ever.

In Super Bowl 50, the Denver Broncos defense finally figured out a way to stop Newton, and Carolina's dream season ended with a loss. But look for Newton's all-around skills to soon find their way back to the NFL's biggest stage.

FAST FACTS!

- Cam had a career-high 35 touchdown passes in 2015.
- His older brother, Cecil, was on the Baltimore Ravens' roster as an offensive lineman in 2015, but didn't make it into any games.
- Cam is one of 14 college players to win the Heisman Trophy and a national championship in the same season.

CAM NEWTON

AARON RODGERS

GREEN BAY PACKERS

QUARTERBACK

		ATTEMPTS:	4,047	TOUCHDOWN PASSES:	25
HEIGHT: 6'2"	COLLEGE: CALIFORNIA	COMPLETIONS:	2,633	RUSHING YARDS:	2,1
WEIGHT: 223	DRAFTED: 2005	PASSING YARDS:	32,399	RUSHING TOUCHDOWNS:	21

NFL passers are remembered for their wins, their stats, and their big plays. For Aaron Rodgers, that's check, check, and check! He's one of the few quarterbacks who combines a great arm, running ability, leadership, and just plain winning. And in 2015, he created a pair of all-time memories.

Rodgers grew up in Northern California. He became a top high school quarterback, but soon learned another important football lesson. He learned about patience. Few big-name schools recruited him, so he spent a year in junior college. After a 10–1 season at Butte College, he got his shot at the big time at California. He ran the Golden Bears' high-scoring offense before moving to the NFL in 2005, when . . . he had to wait again! Rodgers was the backup for the Green Bay Packers behind one of the all-time greats, Brett Favre.

Rodgers watched the future Pro Football Hall of Fame member and learned even more lessons. He knew that eventually he would have big shoes to fill and a lot of fans to make happy . . . fast. Finally, in 2008, Rodgers took over as the starter. A year later, he was in the Pro Bowl. By the 2010 season, he led the Packers to a Super Bowl title. He threw 3 touchdown passes in their 31–25 victory over the Pittsburgh Steelers in Super Bowl XLV and was named the game's MVP. The following season, he also led the NFL with a passer rating of 122.5, which set a single-season record. The key was his low number of interceptions. From 2011

through 2015, Rodgers never threw more than 8 pi in a year. He's not bad running with the ball, either. uses deceptive speed to pick up key first downs—a he's scored 21 career rushing TDs, too!

In 2013, Rodgers showed that he picked up a few lessons in toughness from his old mentor, Favre. After missing seven games with a broken collarbon Rodgers returned for a regular-season-ending showdown with the Chicago Bears for the NFC Nor championship. He passed for 318 yards and 2 TDs. the Packers won the division title!

In 2015, Rodgers and the Packers were part of tw incredibly memorable games. In December, Green trailed the Detroit Lions as time ran out. But a pena on the Lions gave Rodgers one more shot. He sent receivers to the end zone and used his mighty arm heave a 61-yard rainbow. Tight end Richard Rodge (no relation) leaped above a crowd to haul in the miracle game winner.

Aaron had a similar feat in the playoffs. Down by touchdown to the Arizona Cardinals as time wound down, he completed a 60-yard, fourth-down pass t took Green Bay into the Cardinals' territory. Then, the final play of regulation, he found Jeff Janis from yards to tie the game! Unfortunately, the Packers l overtime. (See page 14 to find out how!) With Rod in charge, however, more miracles are certain in th Packers' future.

FAST FACTS!
- Aaron has averaged 32 touchdown passes over his eight seasons as a starter.
- His 104.1 career passer rating is the highest in NFL history.
- He threw 43 TD passes in just two seasons at California.

AARON RODGERS

J. J. WATT

HOUSTON TEXANS

DEFENSIVE END

				TACKLES:	298	FORCED FUMBLES:	15
HEIGHT:	6'6"	COLLEGE:	WISCONSIN	SACKS:	74.5	FUMBLES RECOVERED:	12
WEIGHT:	290	DRAFTED:	2011	INTERCEPTIONS:	1	TOUCHDOWNS:	5

It's pretty rare that the most famous star in the NFL plays defense. But judging from his stack of awards, his outgoing personality, and all the commercials in which he appears, J. J. Watt of the Houston Texans just might have that distinction.

Watt almost didn't get the chance to become a national star. He grew up in Wisconsin, where his first sport was hockey. He was so good as a young player that he was selected for all-star teams that traveled as far as Germany to play. When he was about 13, however, his parents told him that the cost of travel and playing was too much. Disappointed, he turned his athletic talents to football, which he loved to play in his yard with his three brothers. He played for his high school team, but soon had to give up his dream of being a quarterback. He was just too big! He switched to tight end and defensive end as a junior. As he got bigger and stronger, it was clear that knocking people over would be his best skill.

Because he had not played that much, many top schools overlooked him. He went to Central Michigan, where he was a tight end at first. He dreamed, however, of playing for a big school such as the University of Wisconsin. Watt took a huge chance and left Central Michigan to attend Wisconsin without a scholarship. That meant he would have to walk on and prove himself to coaches who did not know if he was

good enough for their team. But the fierce drive he'd shown on rinks and fields in his hometown convince the coaches. He played two seasons at defensive en for the Badgers, and earned the Lott IMPACT Trophy his senior year in 2010 for his combination of on-fie play and personal character.

Needing Watt's high-motor, pass-rushing talent, Houston chose him in the first round of the 2011 NF Draft. Watt wasted no time making his mark on the NFL. He posted 5.5 sacks in his rookie season and helped the Texans make the playoffs. By his second season, he was the NFL Defensive Player of the Year after making 20.5 sacks. He added 10.5 sacks in 20

In 2014, he had another amazing season on both sides of the ball! While racking up 20.5 sacks again, also scored 5 touchdowns! He returned a fumble an an interception for scores. But Houston also put him into goal-line situations on offense as a tight end— remember his high school days?—and he caught 3 touchdown passes. He also won his second NFL Defensive Player of the Year award.

Amazingly, he made it three of those trophies in 2015! He joined former New York Giants great Lawrence Taylor as the only three-time winners . . . and Watt did it in just five seasons!

FAST FACTS!

- In 2014, J. J. was the first player to get all the first-place votes for NFL Defensive Player of the Year.
- He is the only player in NFL history with two seasons of 20 sacks or more.
- He has swatted down 45 passes, the most in the NFL since 2011.

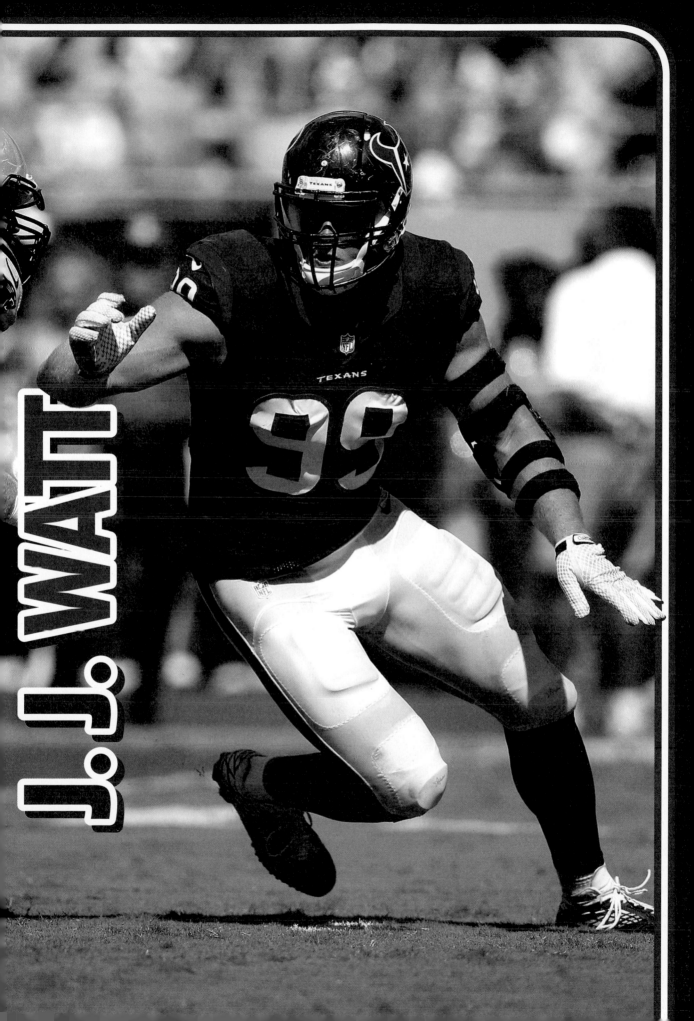

J. J. WATT

Rookie

WHILE **TODD GURLEY** (PAGE 16) IS AT THE TOP OF THE NFL ROOKIE CLASS OF 2015, HERE ARE SOME OTHER YOUNG PLAYERS TO WATCH.

MARCUS MARIOTA

QUARTERBACK • TENNESSEE TITANS

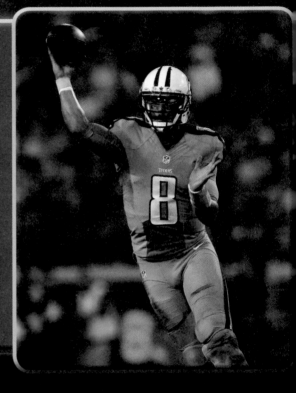

Mariota's debut game in 2015 was just about perfect. In fact, according to the NFL's passer rating system, it was perfect! The No. 2 overall pick of the draft passed for 4 TDs and posted the highest rating possible (158.3) in a 42–14 rout of Tampa Bay. The rest of the season wasn't as flawless, but Mariota still passed for 2,818 yards and 19 touchdowns in only 12 games and gave the Titans hope for the future.

MARCUS PETERS

CORNERBACK •

Rookie defensive backs are usually picked on by veteran NFL passers. They think the "kids" won't know how to handle big-time NFL receivers. Quarterbacks who thought that about Peters made a mistake, as the first-year player tied for the NFL lead in 2015 with 8 interceptions and was named the league's Defensive Rookie of the Year. Peters returned 2 of his picks for touchdowns.

THOMAS RAWLS

RUNNING BACK · SEATTLE SEAHAWKS

Seattle fans were upset when their favorite runner, Marshawn Lynch, went down with an injury in 2015. But their sadness turned to joy when they watched Rawls step into Lynch's big shoes. Rawls was the starter in seven games and had 100 or more yards in four of them, including a masterful 209-yard performance in a victory over the 49ers.

LEONARD WILLIAMS

DEFENSIVE LINEMAN · NEW YORK JETS

Defensive linemen don't usually get much attention from fans unless they rack up a lot of sacks or create memorable sack dances. But some of the best simply clog the middle and make life miserable for offensive linemen and running backs. After the power and strength he showed as a rookie, Williams has a chance to be one of the top defensive linemen in the league.

2015
NFL STANDINGS

AFC

EAST

New England Patriots	12–4
New York Jets	10–6
Buffalo Bills	8–8
Miami Dolphins	6–10

NORTH

Cincinnati Bengals	12–4
Pittsburgh Steelers	10–6
Baltimore Ravens	5–11
Cleveland Browns	3–13

SOUTH

Houston Texans	9–7
Indianapolis Colts	8–8
Jacksonville Jaguars	5–11
Tennessee Titans	3–13

WEST

Denver Broncos	12–4
Kansas City Chiefs	11–5
Oakland Raiders	7–9
San Diego Chargers	4–12

NFC

EAST

Washington Redskins	9–7
Philadelphia Eagles	7–9
New York Giants	6–10
Dallas Cowboys	4–12

NORTH

Minnesota Vikings	11–5
Green Bay Packers	10–6
Detroit Lions	7–9
Chicago Bears	6–10

SOUTH

Carolina Panthers	15–1
Atlanta Falcons	8–8
New Orleans Saints	7–9
Tampa Bay Buccaneers	6–10

WEST

Arizona Cardinals	13–3
Seattle Seahawks	10–6
St. Louis Rams	7–9
San Francisco 49ers	5–11

SUPER BOWL 50: DENVER BRONCOS 24, CAROLINA PANTHERS 10